PLANNING YOUR LIFE

Understanding Yourself and the Person You Want to Become

Richard E. Rusbuldt

Judson Press ® Valley Forge

PLANNING YOUR LIFE

Copyright © 1978
Judson Press, Valley Forge, PA 19481

Unless otherwise indicated, Bible quotations in this volume are in accordance with *The Living Bible* (TLB), Copyright © 1971 by Tyndale House Publishers, Wheaton, Illinois.

Other versions of the Bible quoted in this book are:

the Revised Standard Version of the Bible, copyrighted 1946, 1952, 1971, 1973 © by the Division of Christian Education of the National Council of the Churches of Christ in the United States. Used by permission.

Today's English Version, the *Good News Bible*—Old Testament: Copyright © American Bible Society 1976; New Testament: Copyright © American Bible Society 1966, 1971, 1976. Used by permission.

Library of Congress Cataloging in Publication Data

Rusbuldt, Richard E.
  Planning your life.

  SUMMARY: Presents a program of 12 sessions for the study and planning of life goals. Includes biblical references and suggestions for use of the material in a group setting.
  1. Young adults—Religious life. 2. Young adults—Conduct of life. 3. Youth—Religious life. 4. Youth—Conduct of life. [1. Christian life. 2. Conduct of life] I. Title.
BV4529.2.R87   248'.83   78-8767
ISBN 0-8170-0817-9

The name JUDSON PRESS is registered as a trademark in the U.S. Patent Office. Printed in the U.S.A. ✠

*"If you don't know (or care)
where you're going,
how (or if) you get there
doesn't matter."*

Acknowledgment

To those who assisted by testing this youth life planning material we give a big "THANK YOU." The first group to do this was the "gang" from Centerville Baptist Church, in Centerville, Pennsylvania, including: Lynn, Wendy, Lori, Rick, Dianna, Bert, Lisa, Ed, Stacey, Tammie, Kerrie; counselors were Connie and Gary, Linda and Dick, and Millie and C. E. Depew.

Other groups to test the material and provide us with assistance include Upper Merion Baptist Church, King of Prussia, Pennsylvania; First Baptist Church, Bethlehem, Pennsylvania; and Wayne Park Baptist Church, Erie, Pennsylvania.

My personal thanks to Ms. Betty Sharp for her time spent in reviewing and critiquing the material as it was written and for testing it with several groups. The drawings at the chapter heads were done by Dawn Rusbuldt, a teenager.

Contents

Life Planning—An Overview **9**

Sessions

1 Who Is the Real Me? **13**

2 What Is Important? What Do I Value? **19**

3 Can You Hear What I'm Really Saying? **25**

4 What's Life All About, Anyway? **31**

5 But I Thought . . . ! **35**

6 Some Real Concerns **41**

7 Establishing Personal Goals **45**

8 Setting Some Objectives **49**

9 Action!! **53**

10 Details!! Details!! **57**

11 Some Assistance, Please! **61**

12 How Am I Doing? **65**

Leader's Guide **71**

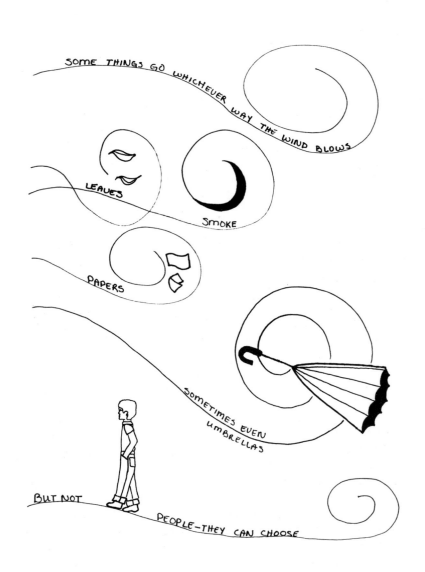

Life Planning—An Overview

Life planning provides an orderly approach to your future. It is an effort to shape your future with confidence using what you know or can learn about yourself and your situation. Some persons ask: "Why bother?"; others feel it's well worth the "bother." Life planning does require time and effort. Take a look at what is involved.

In order to make decisions about your future, begin with the following:

1. Gather all the facts available about yourself.
2. Discover all you can about yourself.
3. Sort out and use this information in your life planning.

Few persons really know themselves well. One of the first steps in life planning is to seek additional information about yourself. The first three sessions in this course use various methods to help you learn more about the real YOU. Much that you learn will confirm what you already know! However, you may also learn some new things about yourself. When you know the real YOU, a solid base on which to build your future is provided.

"What's life all about, anyway?" One of the greatest things that can happen to an individual is to discover purpose in life. Is there purpose (meaning) behind the things you do? Why should you continue to live your life? Is your life worthwhile? Does your life count for anything? Once you identify purpose or mission in life, you provide the framework within which to place everything you do. *(See Session 4.)*

Young people, as well as adults, soon discover that some decisions have long-range effects on their lives. Some decisions, whether good or bad, will have an important bearing on one's life for decades.

In order to make the best decision, gather as many facts as are available about the situation. Important assumptions need to be checked out also. *(See Session 5.)*

Next, consider the options. Many persons, later in life, realize there were more options open to them than they considered when making certain important decisions. It is a wise builder who considers all options. Why build a house utilizing oil, gas, or coal for energy sources when solar energy may be an option? Years from now, the answer to that question will make a vast "world of difference," both in terms of economics and life-style. *(See Session 6.)*

Then work your life plan. The person who puts life goals and objectives in writing will not forget them. They can be reviewed regularly. Some persons say they can do this mentally; experience tells us the human mind can't contain all the details of this type of planning. *(See Sessions 7, 8, 9, 10, 11.)*

Are you locked into the plan forever? Definitely not! One of the joys of planning is being able to take new data, examine what you have written, and make appropriate changes. Goals can be rewritten; objectives can be changed. Life purpose can change, also. Being aware of these changes will help you "work smarter" than the person who has changed purpose or goals but is not really aware of what has happened to him or her. *(See Session 12.)*

Biblical references, both for study and illustration, are included in most of the sessions.

The Leader's Guide in the back of the book contains suggestions for the use of this material in a group setting.

When using this material with a group, you may want to divide your sessions into three sets with four sessions each. Take a break after sessions 4 and 8 to give the participants time to rest and absorb what they have been doing.

If available time is a problem for an individual or a group, Sessions 2, 3, 5, 10, and 12 can be optional. Twelve sessions are needed to give equal treatment to the various aspects of life planning. However, each leader will need to examine each session and determine which can be omitted if available time does not permit the full twelve weeks.

Begin with a Party

Since Life Planning deals with the future, a party about the future is a good way to begin this course. Plan your party with an emphasis on what you guess will be happening fifteen or twenty years from now.

Obviously, not every teen knows what he or she will be doing then. Neither do adults. Almost everyone, however, has hopes and dreams, if not specific plans, about his or her future. At a party, someone who wants to be a nurse can dress in a nurse's uniform and take everybody's blood pressure! A future farmer could come dressed for the part. A bank president could hand out Monopoly-style money all evening. And on and on. If some group members have no idea of what they want to be or do, ask them to use their imagination and select something they feel good about right now.

What can you do at a "Future Party"? Here are some suggestions:

- Futuristic type games; check with the local library, pastor, and teachers for sources.
- The movie *Future Shock* (16 mm sound film, 42 min., rental— $40; available at McGraw-Hill Films) deals with the future; check with the local media teacher.
- Crystal-ball gazing; select someone who knows your group and has a sense of humor to be the gazer. What is shared should be funny and positive, not hurtful.
- Make some slides. Have each person make a slide which might show some of the following: what he or she may look like ten to twenty years from now; what he or she may be doing; where he or she might live; a title he or she might have. Cartoon characters or stick figures can be used. Initial each slide. Show them to the group when all are completed. Slide-making information is available from your local media teacher or your local library or denominational office. Keep the slides for future use.
- Snacks, desserts, favors, etc., can also reflect the future.
- Near the end of the party, talk a bit about some of the things you'll be doing together. Enlist the interest and support of the group for this study.

All participants and leaders may want to sign a contract such as the one on the following page.

Contract for Life Planning Course

I understand this course will last approximately _____ weeks.

I will be present every session, if possible, and complete the course.

Since some outside work is involved, I'll do my best to complete the assignments.

I'll participate in group sessions to the best of my ability.

Group members' signatures _____

_____

_____

As a group leader, I will prepare my sessions in advance of the meetings.

I'll be present at every session, if possible.

I will make myself available for individual work with group members.

I will do my best to make it interesting.

Group leaders' signatures _____

_____

Who Is the Real Me?

This session deals with *three basic questions:*
- How much do I *really* know about myself?
  (Do I know the *real me?)*
- How can I learn *additional* things about myself?
- Can I *"check out"* what I think I already know about myself?

HOW MUCH DO I KNOW ABOUT MYSELF?

Most of us know some hard facts about ourselves—such as, when and where I was born; when I started school; if I like green cheese; my grades for last term; the status of my money supply; etc. However, some other parts of ourselves are not so clear. Less clearly defined parts of our lives get "fuzzy" and appear to be much more complicated.

Ask yourself these questions: Am I an optimist, or am I deep-down inside a pessimist about life? Am I well organized, am I "chaos in person," or am I somewhere in between? What feelings do I display more often than others? Am I basically a kind, concerned person toward others? Do I care about myself? Am I committed to God—to a faith? What does that commitment cause me to do? What does God expect me to do—or be? Does God care? Do my friends care?

Discover more about yourself and you will be better prepared to face your future. A more clear understanding of what makes you "tick" will better prepare you to do some life planning. Also, as you become better acquainted with yourself, you will see many more possibilities for your future.

LEARNING ABOUT MYSELF

Let's take a look at the whole picture of your life. You don't know some things about your life yet; so you'll have to do some guessing. But some things you do know; so concentrate on these. The "big picture" of one's life can be called a *Personal Life Line.* Here's how to proceed.

Personal Life Line

Get a large piece of newsprint and a wide felt-tip pen. If newsprint is not available, get a wide roll of white shelf paper, unroll it, and cut off as much as you need. Allow yourself plenty of space. Make your life line at least three or four feet long if paper permits. You'll work on your life line again in later sessions.

"I AM HERE."

Birth	Top 3 Events of Your Life So Far Date When Happened			#1 Goal in Life	Death
	June, 1961	Learned to walk	Fell June, 1961	June, 1961	Learned to get up June, 1961

Key to Personal Life Line

Birth—Give date when you were born. Where?

Top 3 Events—What are your three greatest events or experiences to date? (They may be positive or negative.) Place the approximate date after each.

#1 Goal in Life—At this moment, what is your Number 1 Goal?

Death—You don't know when you'll die, but take a guess as to when it might be.

"I am here"—In relationship to the birth and death dates, place a vertical line which estimates where you are now on your life line.

List and Interview

The next step is to put in writing what you know about yourself. Then check it out during the next few weeks. Work now on "My Checklist for the Real Me!" which follows. If you don't have time to complete it this session, work on it at home. As soon as it's finished, interview peers or friends of any age, such as parents, youth advisers, teachers, pastor, roommate, employers, etc. The more you interview, the more you'll learn about how others see you. Whether you agree with their insights or not, what you find will be enlightening.

If you interview more than one person in order to check your list, use a separate paper on which to record each one's responses. Be sure to number each item, since you may not want to submit all items on the list to each person interviewed. Share with each person interviewed only those items with which you feel comfortable and about which you feel the person can provide significant feedback. Record a name on each sheet so you will know which person said what.

My Checklist for the REAL Me!

(Unless instructed to do otherwise, make a list under each of the headings below.)

1. My strengths are:

2. My weaknesses are:

3. I value highly:

4. I feel good when I:

5. I feel bad when I:

6. I respect: *(list persons, groups, positions, etc.)*

7. My relationship to God is: *(describe in a sentence)*

8. I like:

9. I don't like:

10. My relationship to my parents is:

11. My relationship to my brothers/sisters is: *(name each and use one or two words to describe each relationship)*

12. My relationship to my church is: *(describe briefly)*

13. I'm afraid of:

14. My image with my peers is: *(state what you think it is)*

15. My image with my parents is: *(state what you think it is)*

16. My talents are:

17. The three most important decisions in my life have been:

18. The two most influential persons in my life today are:

19. I have accomplished the following: *(list whether you feel they are "great" or "small")*

(For Post Highs Only)
20. I feel _____ about what I accomplished in high school.

21. I _____ what I'm doing since high school days.

22. I'm worried about the following these days:

Complete These Sentences
23. Prayer is _____ in my life.

24. My pastor thinks I'm _____ .

25. The future is _____ to me.

26. I hurt most when I _____ .

27. I'm proud of _____ .

28. The people I trust most of all are _____ .

29. I like to be _____ by others.

30. I'm most happy when I _____ .

CHECKING OUT WHAT I FIND

When you've completed checking out your list, select *the one person* in the whole world who knows you better than anyone else and share with that person what you've learned. How does she or he feel about what others have told you and what you've said about yourself? Does the feedback agree with what you thought? Does it differ greatly? If it differs, recheck your list to determine if it's *really* what you think.

———

In closing, study 1 Corinthians 9:24-27 (preferably from *The Living Bible*). Paul was describing life as a race to be won. Anyone who has ever run in any kind of race has to think about the future, sometimes immediate—sometimes long-range. Did Paul find the future exciting? Did he feel it was worth giving 100 percent to get the prize? How did he feel about the future?

Close with prayer.

PIZZA

1st –   GOD

2nd –   RECORDS

3rd –   BOYFRIEND (GIRL)

4th –   CAR

MONEY

What Is Important?
What Do I Value?

This get-together deals with three vital questions:
- What do I value? What is important?
- What have I accomplished to date?
- What is my heritage? (optional)

WHAT DO I VALUE?

Begin this session by discussing what Jesus valued. What did Jesus seem to think important in life? Did he value persons more than things? Did he highly value relationships with others? What values did he offer in the Sermon on the Mount? Was honesty important to Jesus? Make a list of Jesus' values; all members of the group can contribute to the list. When your list is completed, ask yourselves this question: Was his death related in any way to these values? Some verses you might want to look at are:

Matthew 6:24, 31-34; 7:13-14
Luke 10:38-42; 12:31
John 11:35

Before you try to list your own values and what you think is important, complete this exercise:

A devastating flood has just struck your area. You have been warned you have but three minutes to evacuate. You are solely responsible for saving whatever will be saved from your home. You can take with you no more than five things. What will you save?

You have but three minutes to make your list:

_____   _____

_____   _____

_____   _____

Now spend no more than ten minutes working on your own list of what you feel is important to you at this moment in life—your values. Since you will want to give this item serious thought, complete it at home during the week.

WHAT HAVE I ACCOMPLISHED TO DATE?

Many teenagers, as well as adults, tend to minimize their accomplishments. If statues haven't been erected for them, parades held in their honor, or big headlines carried their names, they consider themselves unimportant.

Yet every person makes an impact on others and does some things—whether great or small—which greatly affect the lives of others. Sometimes the impact is great; other times it may be so-so; and of course, there is always a possibility it may be harmful. YOU have affected the lives of many persons. What you did may not have seemed important to you at the time, but it could have been very significant to the other person. Discuss as a group how each of you has made an impact on the life of someone else. Stick to the positive, please!

You've probably heard of the Richter scale. It's used to measure the intensity of earthquakes all over the world. When an earthquake occurs, the world knows whether it is a mild event, an average quake, or a great disaster, by the measurement on the Richter scale. Setting aside the fact that earthquakes can be destructive, and thinking only of the notice the scale gives to the world, try to measure what Jesus did in the last three years of his life. If you were to register Jesus' deeds and accomplishments on a scale like earthquakes are measured, what would you list? What would his personal Richter scale look like? What was Jesus' number 1 accomplishment? What did he do that made "the biggest noise"? What did he do quietly, insignificantly, and without fanfare that brought about significant change? What was his most important contribution to the world? To you? Copy the outline for a Personal Richter Scale for Jesus on newsprint or a chalkboard. As a group, list on the scale seven items from Jesus' life, and then rank them. In the feeling column, use a word which you think Jesus might have used to describe that particular accomplishment.

PERSONAL RICHTER SCALE FOR JESUS

(In this scale, #7 ranks as highest, greatest; #1 is lowest on the scale. In the feeling column, use one word to describe how you think Jesus felt about what he did.)

#	The Event	Feeling
#7		
#6		
#5		
#4		
#3		
#2		
#1		

What would *your* Personal Richter Scale look like? If you were to register your deeds and accomplishments on a scale like this, what would you list? What's your number 1 accomplishment to date? What have you done that's made a "big bang"? Only a few people may know about it, but it can still be a giant-sized accomplishment to you. Perhaps it was something you did for a small child down the street; maybe you did something for your Grandma, a neighbor, a friend, or your parents. A stranger? Someone in need? For God?

Spend a few minutes thinking about your life to date. List seven items on your PERSONAL RICHTER SCALE which greatly affect the lives of others or the course of human events in your home or community. If you can't list seven, that's OK. List what you can.

(In this scale, #7 ranks as highest, greatest; #1 is lowest on the scale. In the age column, give your age when it happened. In the feeling column, use one word to describe how you felt about what you did.)

PERSONAL RICHTER SCALE

#	The Event	Age	Feeling
#7			
#6			
#5			
#4			
#3			
#2			
#1			

WHAT IS MY HERITAGE?

The last step in today's process is to work out your family heritage, or your family roots. What do you know about your family? Your parents? Your grandparents? Your great-grandparents? Each of you is at least partially a product of those who have gone before. They have provided an environment, a setting, and a cultural framework to which you were introduced and in which you have lived. *(If you don't know your parents or their background, write about those who have cared for you, affected you, and provided you with a home, environment, culture, etc.).* Some questions you may want to answer are:

1. What is (was) important to my parents or guardians? What do (did) they value?

2. What important accomplishments have my parents, grandparents, and/or others in my background made that I know about?

3. What feelings do I have about my family roots?

4. What strengths am I aware of that have been in my family or in those who have cared for me?

5. Have God and his church been important to other members in my family tree? Name them and tell how.

Congratulations! As you learn more about yourself, you're getting better acquainted with YOU. You've discovered that you are much more capable, significant, and interesting than you once thought. You're really a great person! Even the God of the universe thinks you're important!

How does this understanding of your values and roots fit into life planning? It may be difficult for you to tell at this point. However, what you value and the people who you think are important greatly affect what you will do with the rest of your life. Rather than "leave it to chance," it's better to understand yourself in terms of what you value and to use this knowledge in making decisions about your future.

As you close today's session, give yourself a pat on the back! Then give every other member in your group a warm hug. Aw, come on—it's not bad! Then dismiss your group by reading together the verses from Matthew 6:25-26 *(The Living Bible)*.

"So my counsel is: Don't worry about *things*—food, drink, and clothes. For you already have life and a body—and they are far more important than what to eat and wear. Look at the birds! They don't worry about what to eat—they don't need to sow or reap or store up food—for your heavenly Father feeds them. And you are far more valuable to him than they are."

Can You Hear What I'm Really Saying?

In this session, three areas of concern are featured:
- How well do I communicate?
- Responsibilities—and me! (Yeah! or Ugh!)
- My faith

By now, you may be wondering why you need to spend so much time learning about yourself. Life is complex. As you grow older, it will become even more complex. Someone has observed: "Life is like an onion; you peel it off one layer at a time, and sometimes you weep." Your life is just like an onion. In order to "get to the inside," you need to keep taking off more layers. Do it with your group—peel an onion—and maybe weep! Then discover how this session tries to peel another layer off to get to the *REAL* you!

HOW WELL DO I COMMUNICATE?

The ability to communicate with others is a skill each one of us needs to develop. Persons can be limited for a lifetime by not being able to communicate clearly. Better jobs, educational opportunities, and self-improvement can disappear when we are unable to say what we mean.

Ask yourself these questions:

— Do people, most of the time, know what I mean when I say something?   Yes _____   No _____

— Am I often misunderstood?   Yes _____   No _____

25

— Do I tend to blame myself _____ others _____ when I am misunderstood?

— In general, is my communication with others of a positive _____ negative _____ nature?

— Do my actions reflect the words I say?   Yes _____ No _____

— Is talking to others easy _____ hard _____ for me to do?

— Do I like _____ not like _____ to talk before a group or class?

Try this fun experience to discover how well you give or receive a communication. You have two options: your total group can participate together, or, divide your group into small groups of three persons and do it.

If you chose the first option and remain as a total group, get two or three volunteers to take turns giving directions on how to draw a diagram. The diagram can be anything they want it to be, such as a square box, with lots of lines crisscrossing it, a series of circles, etc. *(See illustrations below.)* Remember that whatever diagram *you* draw, *you* must then communicate it to the total group.

The person who describes the diagram should get behind a screen or partition or go into an adjoining room. Make sure all can hear. Group members should draw the design that is described to them by "the voice." No questions may be asked of the "describer," except to repeat an instruction. Moans and groans of pleasure or disgust with the directions may be given!

If you chose option two and divide into small groups, form clusters of three persons into what we will call triads. In each triad, one person should describe the diagram; while doing this, he or she should face

Illustrations:

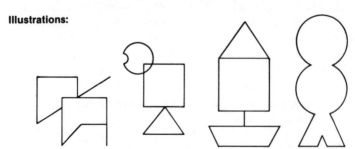

away from the person drawing. Another person should draw the design and the third person will take notes on what he or she observes. These roles can be rotated if time permits.

How well did you communicate? Did the "describer" do a good job? Did you draw what was described? If not, did the "describer" fail, or did the "listener" not listen—or both? How did you feel about your role? Discuss your feelings with your group *(large or small)* for a few minutes.

RESPONSIBILITIES

(This section is for senior highs only—post highs move to the third area of concern, "My Faith."

Our second concern for this session is carrying out responsibilities. No one in this world escapes the clutches of responsibility on some level. Some persons seem to thrive on responsibility and want to get more. Others shy away from additional responsibilities and have great difficulty with what they already have.

Which do you do? You are most likely a much more responsible person than you think you are. You can prove it, too. Fill out the following questions, including all types of responsibilities, such as burning the papers at home, cleaning your room, serving as an usher at church, helping your friend with homework, tutoring a child, etc. Consider nothing you do as trivial when you make your list of responsibilities.

Three columns are provided after each responsibility you list. Check the feeling that applies to that item. The columns are titled: "I like it"; "So-so"; "I don't like it." (See next page).

MY FAITH

(This section is for senior highs and post high youth.)

Our third area of concern is *faith.* What do you believe? Is your faith adequate for where you are in life now? Do you feel good about your faith? Does it bring satisfaction to you? What do you believe about God? What do you wonder about God? The universe? Has your faith been sufficient to "get you through" what you've faced in life thus far?

Faith is personal; only you know what yours is all about. However, what you believe always becomes visible, one way or another.

When you discuss your faith, you are probably sure of some things, but have doubts about others. What part of your faith gives you confidence? Of what are you positive? Also, what do you wonder about your faith?

In the listing below, there are a number of categories which refer to a person's faith, church, religious life, etc. Check the appropriate column for each item. At the end of the printed list, add others which are significant to you in either column.

There is an interesting verse in Matthew 17:20 *(The Living Bible)* which says:

"For if you had faith even as small as a tiny mustard seed you could say to this mountain, 'Move!' and it would go far away. Nothing would be impossible."

A mustard seed is very small, no bigger than the one pictured right here: . Yet, in spite of its size and apparent insignificance, Jesus said that faith that size could do giant things. What size is your faith? Discuss the concept of the mustard seed before you dismiss.

	I like it	So-so	I don't like it
• My school responsibilities are:			
• Responsibilities with my peers are:			
• Responsibilities to myself are:			
• Family or home responsibilities are:			
• Job responsibilities are:			
• Church responsibilities are:			
• Community responsibilities are:			
• Personal responsibilities with God are:			

Related to My Faith	I Know What I Believe About This	I Wonder About This
God		
The Bible		
Jesus Christ		
God in the world		
Salvation		
The Holy Spirit		
Prayer to God		
Witnessing to others about my faith		
God and my future		
God cares for me		
God answers prayer		
The Bible is truth		
My faith will carry me through difficult times		
God has faith in me		
God has a purpose for me in this world		
God will help me find that purpose		

What's Life All About, Anyway?

Young and old ask this question more than once during a lifetime. This session will help you look at several sides of the question. Toward the end of the session, you will have an opportunity to consider personally what your life is all about.

Consider the following:

- An older person says: "Life's just not worth living anymore."
- A young person asks: "Doesn't anybody care at all?"
- A middle-aged person laments: "This job is so boring!"
- A post-high says: ". . . but I can't find a job that's satisfying."
- Jesus said: "Do not start worrying about things—food, drink, and clothes. . . ."
- A teenager says: "I don't know what I want to do."
- The writer of Ecclesiastes says: "There is nothing new under the sun."
- An adult says: "I can't make ends meet anymore."
- *You* ask: "What's life all about, anyway?"

Have you heard other statements or questions about life itself? Have your friends expressed how they feel about life? As a group, discuss what the above statements and questions mean.

The question "What's life all about, anyway?" can be asked another way. You can ask, "What's your mission in life?" or "What's your purpose in life?"

A person's mission in life is simply the answer to the question: "Why should you continue to live and work out your life?" Your life purpose states *"why you're doing* what you're doing," rather than *what* you *are* doing." People spend a lot of time and energy doing things, running here and there, being busy; little time is spent thinking about why they do them.

As a group, select several of the role-play illustrations (if time permits) and act them out.

1. "My purpose in life is to make money." You've probably heard more than one person make this statement. Maybe you feel that way yourself. However, "making money" is in the "doing" category. Find out why a person wants to "make money," and you'll probably discover what is his or her life purpose.

As an example, one person might want to "make money" with which to purchase all kinds of things. Life purpose might include being famous, wealthy, powerful, better off than anybody else, or to have attention, etc. Another might want to "make money" in order to help people in need; in other words, money would be "made" in order to give it away. This person's life purpose might include being called to "a servant role," to help people in need.

(Select one or two persons for each of the positions; "push" each position to its extreme.)

2. The writer of Genesis tells the story of creation. The account indicates that God performed acts of creation on six days and rested on the seventh. What was God's purpose in doing all this? Why did he create the world and put us here? Do you think God is involved in what is happening here on planet Earth?

(Select someone to take God's position; then select several others to deny that there is any divine purpose in the universe.)

3. Two students are attending medical school. Both will soon graduate and serve as doctors. One student says the only place to set up practice is in the suburbs where people and money are in good supply and where a good service can be rendered. The other student says the place to serve as a doctor is in a remote location in Appalachia where there are many persons in need, but few have resources to pay for medical help.

(Select one or two persons to speak for the position of each of the medical students. What is the mission in life for each of them? Is anything wrong with either of them?)

There is a drawing of an empty table to the right of the page. Think for a moment about all that you are doing. This includes school, home, friends, extracurricular activities, jobs, and more. Write on the table all the things in which you are involved.

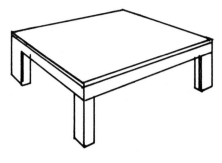

Look them over and ask yourself the questions:
   "Why am I doing all of this?"
      "What's my purpose behind all that I'm doing?"
         "What's my mission in life?"
Purpose implies meaning in life.
   YOU . . . take up space.
   YOU . . . use some of the world's resources.
   YOU . . . affect others . . .

                              WHY?

Life purpose means:
   • I have a mission in life.
   • I have a reason(s) why I should continue to live.
   • Life is worthwhile.
   • Life itself has meaning.
   • When things go wrong, I won't quit.
   • I'll keep on pushing and fighting, in spite of difficulties, obstacles, "brick walls," etc.

Being a Christian provides an additional dimension to life purpose. A Christian's relationship with God implies a purpose beyond self. A caring, loving God can provide you with a "reason for being" beyond yourself. From your group's knowledge of the Bible, select one Old Testament and one New Testament personality who had a purpose or mission in life. Discuss these persons, first identifying what they did, and then, why they did it *(their purpose or mission)*.

Now identify two persons you personally know who have found meaning and purpose in life. What are they doing? Why are they doing it? What is their "reason for being"? What are the "driving forces" (purpose or mission) which keep them going, especially if they have great obstacles to overcome? Share the "what" and the "why" of these persons with your group.

1. Name:
   What he or she is doing:
   Why?

2. Name:
   What he or she is doing:
   Why?

Writing a life-purpose statement takes much thought and is not easy. In fact, some people find it almost impossible to do. However, it's worth a try. Work on your statement now. If you can't write one now, keep it in mind; think about it, and perhaps in the days and months ahead, you'll be able to do it. Also remember that when you're young, your purpose may change from time to time. You're not "locked in" to whatever statement you write now.

One last reminder: Your purpose or mission in life is *why* you are doing what you are doing. (Not *what* you are doing!) For the Christian, mission or purpose comes from God. If this is true for you, then God's will becomes basic to your statement.

Session 5

But I Thought . . . !

"But I thought—
  ". . . you bought the tickets for the game!"
  ". . . I had the right-of-way!"
  ". . . *I* was your boy/girl friend!"
In the situations described above, each person had made an "assumption" and found out he or she was most likely wrong. Assumptions seem to "pop up" in the strangest places and at most unusual times.

WHAT ARE ASSUMPTIONS?

Assumptions can be made about people, things, situations—even the future itself. You make many assumptions in the course of an ordinary day. It would be impossible to check out all of them. But as you mature, you will learn that you must be very careful when making certain assumptions. If you are wrong, there can be serious consequences—sometimes to yourself, sometimes to others. Just what is an assumption?
  An assumption is:
  - something I'm counting on, but it's out of my control.
  - something I can't prove but am willing to act on.
  - an outcome I'm not sure of, but I'd be willing to bet on.
  - feeling certain something will happen but not knowing "for sure."
  - a feeling I have about the future, but I can't prove.
  - a "gut level" hunch about something.

Here are three situations which contain assumptions. Discuss each one as a group (if you have enough time). List the assumptions on newsprint so you can compare all three.

Situation 1:

"It's the biggest game of the year. Your team and your arch-rival play for the league championship. The teams are evenly matched and have lost but one game each. It's not raining. You're playing at home. You have the best quarterback in the league. This is the last game for ten of your players."

What assumptions might be made about this situation by—
   the fans?
   the coach?
   the quarterback?
   the hot-dog concession?
   the other team?

Situation 2:

"A fellow named Moses was 'skeedaddlin' out of Egypt with a gang of people runnin' all over the place. They'd been told to get out of Egypt, like fast. But the people had to leave in such a hurry they were mighty upset by all that was going on. Besides that, Moses wouldn't really tell them where they were going. He acted like he didn't even know. Fact was, he stopped for a map at the last gas station going out of Egypt. They told him that, the price of gas being what it was, they couldn't give maps anymore. Some of the folks knew that up ahead was a body of water. That didn't make them feel very good, either. Some of them thought Moses had 'slipped a cog.'

"While all this was happening, Moses turned around and saw dust rising off in the distance. He knew then that the Pharaoh had changed his mind. Moses acted quickly to get the people to move faster. Would the Egyptians catch them? What would happen when Moses and his people hit the Red Sea?"

What assumptions might be made about this Bible story by—
   Moses?
   the Israelites?
   the Pharaoh?
   the Egyptian soldiers?

Situation 3:

"You attend high school. You are expected to maintain passing grades and graduate in a certain number of years. To do this, you are supposed to study, attend classes regularly, behave, pass all courses, do homework regularly, etc."

What assumptions might be made about this situation by—

you, the student?

your parents?

the teachers?

society, in general?

Assumptions are a part of daily living. However, when a situation arises which has great bearing on your future, it's wise to check out each of your assumptions. In order to check out assumptions, search for all the available facts you can find. When you have all the "hard facts" you can discover, then make your decision. Checking out an assumption takes time. However, it's well worth it.

Here are some illustrations of assumptions made and not checked out.

1. You want to get a full-time job when you graduate from high school. In your local community is a factory, Ajeks Couplings, which you've known all your life. You'd like to work there. You're counting on getting a job there. Finally you graduate. You go to the factory to apply for a job. It's closed. The sign says they are bankrupt. The job you counted on was gone.

(One assumption, among others, was that the factory would be employing people when you graduated. You could have interviewed company leaders in your junior-senior year and collected data from them.)

2. You've always wanted to teach elementary children in public school. You make plans to go to college for this purpose. You go to college and prepare to be an elementary school teacher. You graduate and discover there is a huge surplus of teachers in this field. You can't find a teaching job. You're now driving a taxi.

(The assumption was that plenty of jobs for elementary teachers or, at the least, one for you would be available. You could have discussed the market for elementary teachers while you were a sophomore. This would have provided you with more options. You could then have taught other things until the day came when you could be an elementary teacher.)

3. You want to go to college. You always have. Your family doesn't have a lot of money, but you're not poor, either. Since four years of college will be somewhat expensive for you, you're counting on Mom and Dad to put you through. Also, you'll get a job. When

you are a senior in high school, your mom and dad get a divorce. Both of their situations are such that they will be able to provide little help.

(There are several assumptions here. First, you assumed that Mom and Dad would be able to help you get through college. Now they're divorced, and, depending on the situation, you may not have had any way to check this out. A second assumption is that you could go to college only if they remained married. This now needs to be checked out, since other sources of support may be available to you that weren't before.)

Assumptions come in various sizes and shapes. Some can be funny; some are very serious. For instance—

• Funny: A guy and a gal, madly in love, were in a crowded theater lobby waiting for the mob to begin to move. There was a great deal of pushing, shoving, and general movement. After a long wait, they were told there would be further delay. The guy had been standing just in front of his gal. Intent on getting into the theater, he half turned his head and said to her, "Darling, it's worth all of this just to be with you." The guy in back of him said, "Thanks . . . but I don't really feel that way about you."

(The assumption: His girl friend was standing in back of him. In the jostling she had lost her place behind him. He hadn't checked it out.)

• Headachy: A youth group traveled to Philadelphia for an evening event. Thirty-six teens and adults were transported by seven cars. When the event was over, the members of the group were allowed to ride back in any car they wanted, as long as each driver knew he or she had the correct number of persons. At 11:30 that night, the Philadelphia police called the group leader to tell him that Chip was still in the city—would someone come and get him? Chip got home after 2:30 A.M.!!

(The assumption: That all thirty-six persons were in the seven cars.)

• Dangerous: While fishing in Canada, two fishermen pulled their boat next to an island. They'd been fishing for quite a while. Their legs were stiff, and they wanted to stretch and walk. One fisherman stepped out of the boat onto the island and disappeared under the water! They had stopped beside one of the "floating islands" found in certain lakes in Canada.

(The assumption: The island they were going to get on was solid ground.)

• Have Long-Term Effects: Some young people and adults smoke cigarettes. Health agencies say smokers get cancer much more than nonsmokers. You decide to smoke. Years later you get cancer.

(The assumption: You would be in the percentile of those smokers who did not get cancer.)

Now make a list of assumptions about your group which illustrate each of the four categories: Funny, Headachy, Dangerous, and Have Long-Term Effects.

CHECKING OUT YOUR ASSUMPTIONS

Many of your assumptions are "unconscious." That means many of them are so much a part of your daily life that you have neither the time nor the inclination to sort and check them out. In life planning, you should be concerned about major assumptions on which a great deal of your future depends. Check out each assumption on which you base a great amount of your future.

What are your personal assumptions about the future? Think about your personal life and current situation. Write down some of the major assumptions you have or are making.

To assist you, here are some categories to use in writing them. *(Examples are given for each).*

• My Faith.   These assumptions pertain to what I believe. What does my faith say to me about my future?

   Example: God exists and cares personally about me.

   Example: God has a plan for my life.

• My World. These assumptions pertain to my home, peers, school, job, etc. Also included are matters of worldwide importance which may affect me.

   Home example: Mom and Dad will provide me with support and guidance through my teen years.

   School example: My current scholastic efforts in school will be sufficient to meet my needs in adult life.

   Job example: I'll get the job I want when I finish school.

   World or energy example: There will always be gasoline to drive my car.

• My way of Doing Things. These assumptions include how I get things done, perform tasks, accomplish what I set out to do, etc.

   Example: My effective schoolwork will help me get a job. My good school record will get me into the college of my choice.

After you have written some assumptions, place a check beside each one that needs to be checked out. Checking out an assumption won't guarantee its accuracy; however, you can learn everything about it that is possible, thus lessening the probability of being wrong in the assumption you have made.

Some Real Concerns

So far in this course, you've:
- learned some things about yourself;
- worked on your life purpose;
- noted some assumptions.

Only one step remains before you decide what goals you want for your life. Life goals emerge from your concerns. An *area of concern* is something from the "mix of your life" which calls, compels, or speaks so strongly that you *must* act. These areas of concern may include such things as problems, issues, needs, opportunities, and challenges.

Areas of concern may focus on yourself or other persons and situations. In other words, the concern may be personal and the goal which results will be directed inward; or, the concern may be related to your community, your church, or the environment. The following categories may help you sort your areas of concern:

Problems—Problems are conditions which need to be solved. What are you aware of in your life to date that you'd like to invest some of your life in solving?

Needs— Needs are situations which require relief and to which *you* can respond because of some special talents, expertise, or interest. Needs touch individuals, families, organizations, churches, even the environment; also age-level, economic, ethnic, and cultural groups. Needs can be local or worldwide. Have you discovered any needs about which you have a burning desire to do something?

Issues—   Issues are situations in life about which persons have taken positions, pro or con. Have you taken sides on any issue to which you'd like to commit some part of your life?

*Opportunities/Challenges—*There are some things around "just waiting for somebody to do them." They won't happen until someone takes the initiative to respond. Are you aware of any challenges you'd like to accept?

Every person has areas of concern. You know people who are concerned about many things; you also know others who have only a few concerns or perhaps just one concern in life. Whether or not you do anything about your areas of concern is strictly *your* business. Others can encourage you to do this or do that, but *you* are the person who decides what and how much you will do.

Sometimes one situation will contain most of the categories of concern. Read the story of Peter in prison, found in Acts 12:1-18.

As a group, answer the following questions:

—Did Peter have a problem(s)? If so, what was it? Did it need to be solved? Could he solve it himself? Did others in the story have problems?

—Did the situation require relief for Peter, others? If so, what kind of relief was needed?

—What were the *real* issues in this story?

—What opportunities or challenges were available to Peter? What doors were opened for him?

After you have completed this discussion, place on newsprint the areas of concern for your group. You have (in most cases) been working together for six weeks. What problems do you now have as a group? Have you discovered any needs that your group has? That others have? Have you faced any issues together? What challenges or opportunities do you see on the horizon for your group? List on newsprint all areas of concern for your group.

You will need some Tinker Toys or building blocks for this exercise. Place on a table one piece of Tinker Toy or a building block for every item you placed on newsprint. If you listed ten areas of concern, place ten toys or blocks on the table. Now as a group, from the assortment of toys or blocks construct something on which you agree and of which you can be proud.

How did you feel doing this? Was there a purpose in what you were doing? Did the pieces fit together? Were there enough? Was the final product worth anything? Did you feel good about what you built?

Conclude this session by writing your personal concerns. Put in writing the problems that "bug" you, whether personal or otherwise. List issues about which you'd like to do something. What mountain (challenge) would you like to climb? List all of the concerns you can think of, whether great or small.

When you've competed your list, pick out the top six. Some will not be as important as others. Select the top six, and then rank them. When you have finished this session, be sure you know your number one area of concern.

Establishing Personal Goals

A personal goal expresses an accomplishment or a long-range result you hope to achieve. In other words, you describe an "end-state" which will exist if the goal is reached. Each goal you write should focus on one major accomplishment you hope to achieve. In most cases, goals have a long-range quality about them. They are not often accomplished in a matter of days or weeks. You may need a number of years to reach a goal.

If you have established a purpose or mission in life, your goals should flow from that purpose. Goals which do not reflect life purpose will be difficult to achieve, frustrating, and counterproductive.

WHAT IS A GOAL?

Goals come in different shapes and sizes, depending on the person who is establishing them. At one point in high school I had a goal to be a concert pianist. That was the end-state. I felt that when I was playing concerts in Carnegie Hall and other places, my goal would be reached. That goal stayed with me for several years, but it didn't work out. (You should have heard me play!) So I set it aside. Prior to the concert pianist goal I had another goal—to be a missionary in Africa. That didn't work out, either. Don't be afraid to set up goals; live with them for a while; and then discard them if they become unrealistic, lose their flavor, or don't reflect your life purpose.

Here is an exercise for your group to use to test your understanding of what a goal should be. Read the following illustration and try your hand at writing a goal statement related to it.

Suppose on a warm and sunny day you arrive at the shore of a beautiful lake. You hear that across the lake, beyond reach by car, is a scenic waterfall. To see this sight, one must go to the other side of the lake. You decide to see the waterfall. After making some inquiries you discover there are rowboats, canoes, and motorboats for rent. Upon further checking, you find that an excursion boat crosses the lake at frequent intervals. Besides all these possibilities, you are a good swimmer and happen to have your bathing suit along!

When you've agreed on a goal statement, ask these questions: Does your statement contain anything about your need to get to the other side of the lake? Does it say anything about the means of transportation for crossing the lake? It shouldn't.

As a nation, we now face energy problems. They will be around for some time. What would be a good goal for our country? We could investigate supplies under the ocean. We can develop solar energy. Coal may be part of the solution. There are many other suggestions. However, these suggestions and statements are not goals. The end-result many have suggested is a nation that is independent of others for energy supplies. Such a goal will stretch us, and time alone will tell whether we reach it or not. However, if that is our goal, it should be what we strive after with all our resources.

Discuss your local church for a moment. What are the goals of your home church? What is your congregation trying to accomplish? Do you have stated goals which you and your congregation know and understand? If not, write some goals toward which you'd like to see your church working. What are the goals of your class or group? Do you have any? If not, why not? Could you write some?

WRITING YOUR GOAL STATEMENT

Goals should emerge from the concerns you identified in the previous session. Remember that a concern is something you feel so strongly about, you *must* act on it in some way. A goal that emerges from a concern such as this will loom very important in your life. Take your number one concern and study it for a while. What kind of goal could you write that would help you do something about that concern? Some sample concerns and goals are suggested in the drawing.

Now write a goal statement for your number one concern. Do the same with some of the other concerns you rated very highly. The average person should deal with no more than four or five goals at a time.

My Goal Is: that I be a physical therapist.

Concern: I'm concerned about the physically handicapped, the crippled, etc.

Concern: Many elderly persons are lonely, have insufficient good food, etc.

My Goal Is: that I be a social caseworker, or to be a registered nurse and work in a nursing home, or to be a local church visitor to the elderly.

Concern: The gospel of Jesus Christ needs to be shared more and in different ways.

My Goal Is: ...That I become a minister of the gospel, or ...that my life-style reflect Jesus' teachings.

Concern: I've never had much money.

My Goal Is: to be a millionaire.

Concern: That solar energy should be developed and utilized wherever possible.

My Goal Is: To be a research engineer in the solar energy field.

Some of the sample goals reflect a vocational thrust, while others point to a style of everyday life. Yet they can all be identified as goals.

Some guidelines for writing a good goal are:
- Be clear in what you say. Don't make it any more difficult than it needs to be.
- If your goal has more than one main point, use more than one goal statement. Have only one point (or focus) for each goal statement.
- Be sure your goal statement says only what the final result (end-state) will be, not how you will reach it. Do not include what you will do to achieve your goal.

- Be concise. Make the statement brief.
- Your goals should be challenging, yet realistic. Don't make them so easy that you will not be motivated to work toward them, nor so gigantic that you will be frustrated.

After you have written your goal statements, get out your *Personal Life Line* which you worked on in Session 1. As you establish each goal, place it in the general time slot during which you will work on that goal. In other words, between the "You Are Here" line and the time you guessed you might die, place your goals in the general time period you want to accomplish them.

What's the target?

Session 8

Setting Some Objectives

Pretend there is a huge, giant-sized boulder in your yard. It weighs at least a half ton. You want to get rid of it. Your goal is to have your yard free of the boulder. Yet you can't lift it; neither can you push it, pull it, or move it sideways to get it out of there. You don't have money to hire a huge crane to pick it up and carry it away. One way to reach your goal is to break the rock into smaller pieces in order to handle it.

You have now arrived at what is called writing objectives. You need to write objectives with which to accomplish your goal(s). By "breaking down a goal," your chances of reaching it will be greater.

An objective is a clear, simple statement of a target or a result at which you aim in order to reach the goal. Objectives should be stated so they can be measured. In this way, you can test movement toward achieving the goal to which it is related.

Ask these questions about each objective:

—Who is to be involved or helped? *(Me, someone else, or both?)*
—How many? How much?
—Where?
—When? *(Beginning when? Accomplished when?)*

Your objectives should answer most of these questions. A good objective also has an *action verb,* such as break, write, build, sing, design, tutor, etc. Avoid vague or general action verbs, such as understand, serve, grow, etc.

Let's go back to the rock. There it sits—too big for you to handle. However, moving it is possible if you can break the rock into smaller pieces. An objective might be: "Within six weeks, break the giant boulder into one hundred smaller rocks which I can move." To break the rock into one hundred smaller rocks becomes the target. One hundred smaller rocks lying around your lawn is the result. You don't need to deal with how you're going to break up the boulder at this point. Moving the pieces will be handled with other objectives.

Usually you can find more than one objective with which to reach a goal. Also, objectives can be classified by the time period you need to achieve them. Short-term objectives need two years or less for completion; long-term objectives are those which take more than two years. A person needs a mix of both short- and long-term objectives when looking at his or her future.

On the basis of what you now know about goals and objectives, try your hand at some examples. Would you classify the following as a goal or an objective?

"Every child shall be able to read."

Answer: _____

If you said it is an objective, sorry about that; it is a goal. It is a general statement with many interpretations.

If you said "objective," why was the answer incorrect? Does the statement tell you specifically what kind of reading performance the child will have? Not really—just that he or she will be able to read. Does the statement tell you when the child will learn to read? No. See how this statement does not *specify exact outcome.*

Here's another example. Is it a goal or an objective?

"To enable every first grade child to learn to read."

Answer: _____

If you said "goal," you were right. Once again, the statement is too general to be a good objective. If you said "objective," take another look at the statement. Does it tell you when the child will learn to read, or what kind of book the child will read?

Yet another example:

"Within one year, each ten-year-old child will be able to read at least 100 fifth-grade-level words per minute with a 70 percent retention rate."

Answer: _____

Now if you said "objective," you are right. The statement clearly specifies the "who" (which children—the ten-year-olds); it also states "how well" or "how much" they will be able to read (100 fifth-grade-level words per minute with a 70 percent retention rate); also the "when" (within one year). A useful objective states a specific result in terms you can measure and tells when the result will take place.

In summary, your objective should answer these three questions:
1. Is the target (intended result) clear?
2. Can you measure it?
3. Does your objective have a time frame?

An interesting exercise using the Bible might be helpful. Read the passage that tells the story of the feeding of the five thousand (found in John 6:1-13). The goal is clear: Jesus and the disciples wanted five thousand persons to be hungry no longer. Write a short-term objective for Jesus and the disciples. Answer the following questions in your objective:

Who needed to be fed?

Who was going to have to do it?

How many needed to be fed? How much food was needed?

Where would they find the food?

How much time did they have to find the food?

That wasn't too hard, was it? Without the miracle performed by Jesus, the "how many" and "how much" would have been much more difficult! That really made it easy!

Now try your hand at writing some objectives. Your leader is available to provide assistance. Work in pairs and help each other if you'd like. Always list your goal and its related objectives so they stay together. The form on the next page may help you.

Life Planning
Area of Concern
Goal #1
Objective #1
Objective #2
Objective #3

Area of Concern
Goal #2
Objective #1
Objective #2
Objective #3

Area of Concern
Goal #3
Objective #1
Objective #2
Objective #3

Etc., Etc.

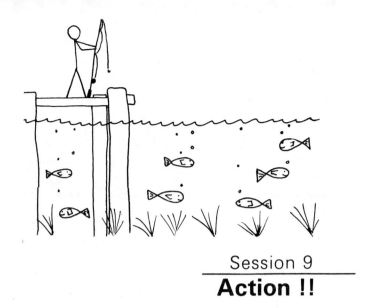

Session 9
Action !!

Now you have some goals and objectives. You know what you are aiming at. You know what results you want. The question now is: "How can I accomplish them?" Speaking in California just before he died, Abraham Maslow said, "The only happy people I know are those who are working hard at something they think is important." (Not something your friends or parents think is important.) If *you* think what you're doing is important, you'll work twice as hard to get it done!

What's the best way to accomplish an objective? By creating some *Action Plans*.

An *Action Plan* is a blueprint which, in general, describes how you can use what you have to achieve an objective. It's a "skeleton outline" of something you will do to reach the objective. You need to pick the most promising way to reach the objective. In order to do this, you need to look at all the alternatives.

Don't look at the success stories of other people in order to find a blueprint for your own success. The quest for your happiness and satisfaction in life will come when you find *your own* unique plans and establish *your own* unique priorities. Erik Erikson, professor emeritus of Harvard University, didn't find it necessary to have a high school diploma. Albert Schweitzer left Europe and the world of academia, the world of music and fine instruments, the world of culture, to find his destiny in the most primitive part of Africa.

There are lots of ways to get things done. Let's take a goal that was mentioned earlier in Session 7 for a fun illustration: "My goal in life is to be a millionaire." Let's say you wrote an objective that reads something like this: "By the time I am thirty years old, I will acquire stocks, bonds, and savings accounts which total one million dollars." Since you own no stocks or bonds and have only $25.11 in your savings account, this becomes a rather significant, challenging task. How are you going to do it? How can you reach this objective?

There are quite a few ways to reach the objective. It is extremely important that you look at every option open to you before you choose the best Action Plan. Break into small groups with three persons in each and brainstorm* for five minutes on the best possible ways to achieve this objective. What plans will work best to "make you a millionaire"?

How did you come out? Compare the lists from your small groups. It is always helpful to get all the contributions that you can from other persons in order to get the best ideas. Often the best idea for an Action Plan is not obvious to you but may be quite visible to someone else. *(If you're short on ideas for becoming a millionaire, your leader has a list in the Leader's Guide you may want to check out.)*

Let's try another one. You are a Christian and belong to a church somewhere. You fully believe in the worth of the Christian church, and you want it to succeed. You feel the church is meeting the needs of many persons, and you want it to continue to do so. You believe the gospel should not only be preached but also should be expressed by all members of your congregation in many settings. You believe in the work of the church so strongly that you write this objective: "During the first five years of my 'twenties' (age 20-25), I will make one (or two) significant contribution(s) to my church." *(For some Action Plan suggestions see the end of this session.)*

How can you accomplish this objective? What can you do that will fulfill your objective? What would be the *best* blueprint to get this done? What is the most significant Action Plan you can write? Again, in small groups, work this one through, using the brainstorming method. When you have compared your lists, decide as a total group what could be your most significant contribution in that five-year period.

Now try to write your own Action Plans. Work in the same small groups. Take your number one goal, and select the most important objective for that goal. Now try to find the best Action Plan for that

---

*Brainstorming off the top of the head is the spontaneous outpouring of ideas related to a specific topic. For a limited time (5 minutes) participants present their ideas freely. Each idea is written on newsprint or chalkboard exactly as it is offered *without being modified* in any way. The ideas don't have to be related to each other at all.

objective. Answer the question: "What is the best way to reach this objective?" Do this for each person in your group.

If the size of your group permits, it would be well worth the time to brainstorm every person's objective. In this way, each of you can make a significant contribution to every other person in your group. However, a lack of time may permit only brainstorming in your small groups.

The gospel is Good News for everyone, including young people. Do you believe God has some plans for your life? What does the gospel say to you about your Action Plans?

Prayer is one of the most meaningful ways to approach your future. Talk to God and discuss your feelings, anxieties, hopes, and dreams; seek his guidance as you make your Action Plans.

Possible Action Plans for the Objective Relating to the Church.

—I will select and carry out a project for my church.
—I will join the choir.
—I will become a counselor with the youth group.
—I will start a program for the elderly.
—I will volunteer to serve as a board member.
—I will become a tither and give 10 percent of my earnings to the church.
—I will become a volunteer, short-term missionary for two years.
—(Other)

A snail was climbing slowly up a cherry tree when a beetle spied him and called out:

Beetle: Hey! There aren't any cherries on that tree.

Snail: I know, but there will be by the time I get up there.

Details!! Details!!

Details!! Who likes details? Some people do . . . but a lot of people don't!! Taking care of details is time consuming and often a headache; but it's "details that make the world go round." When details are not properly handled, some part(s) of your personal life can be in a "shambles." You know some persons right now whose lives are mixed up because some important details have been neglected or ignored.

We said earlier that an Action Plan was a blueprint for building. Study a blueprint. You will see lines which mark the frame of a building, rooms within the building, halls and corridors, doorways, etc. In small print, you will see many figures and instructions. These are the details. They tell you that the doorway should be three feet wide, not four feet; that it should be in the left wall, not the right wall; that there are to be three electrical outlets in the room, not just one, etc. A building project requires this detailed set of blueprints and a construction schedule. In the same way Action Plans require specific descriptions of activities and a schedule for doing what is planned.

Consider the Old Testament story of Noah and the ark. Before you read the Scripture related to it, you might want to listen to Bill Cosby's story about Noah. Then read the passages from Genesis 6:5-22; 7:1-10. God's Action Plan was to build an ark. One of the details was that Noah was the builder. Obviously, an ark can be big, medium, or small. God gave Noah a lot of details about size, including height, width, etc. Noah also received specific instructions about the animals. Together, list all the details you can from the story. What could have gone wrong if some of the details had not been carried out?

Action Plan details provide a complete description of: (1) what is to be done; (2) who will be involved; (3) what the assignments are; (4) the target dates when the work on the details will begin and be completed, as well as the dates when you will check your progress; and (5) the changes that are intended.

The following are the parts you should include as details of an Action Plan:

1. Always list the Objective and a statement which describes its related Action Plan at the top of your worksheet.
2. *Who* will be involved in making this happen? (In most cases, you will be the person, but there may be times someone else will be involved. Identify the "who.")
3. *When* will this happen? (When will the events of the Action Plan begin? When will they be finished?)
4. *Where* will this happen? (And under what conditions?)
5. *How* will this happen? (What will you, and others, *do* to make this happen?)
6. *What* specifically *will be different or changed* if "what happens" is successful? (If something good, constructive, or meaningful isn't going to happen, the plan may not be worth doing. Describe what will be different.)

Some guidelines for writing Action Plans are:

1. Be realistic about the amount of time you have to carry out the details of your Action Plan.
2. Communicate directly and clearly with any other persons who may be involved in carrying out the Action Plan details.
3. Create your blueprint, including the parts listed above.
4. Be careful not to skip details. Double-check each one.
5. Decide how often you will measure your progress while you carry out the Action Plan.

Each Action Plan should have its own set of details. A suggested format for your details worksheet follows. Work your Action Plan through the details as you conclude this session.

ACTION PLAN WORKSHEET

Objective: _____

_____

Action Plan: _____

_____

Action Plan Details:

- *Who* will make this happen? _____

_____

- *When* will this happen? (Begin? End?) _____

_____

- *Where* will this happen? _____

_____

- *How* will this happen? _____

_____

_____

_____

_____

- *What* will be different or changed? _____

_____

_____

_____

_____

Some Assistance, Please!

When business or industry has a plan or project it intends to complete, someone is always placed in charge of the plan. In a hospital, each floor, wing, or ward is under the watchful eye of a supervisor. Education, government, and institutions have learned that the best way to complete a plan is to assign responsibility. A specific person needs to see that the details of the plan are carried out.

In life planning, the role of the Action Plan manager is that of an "enabler"—one who helps another person get things done. The "helper" role can be extremely meaningful. It is often the difference between completing or not being able to complete an Action Plan.

An Old Testament story illustrates the point. Read Exodus 17:8-16, where the story of Israel's fight with Amalek is recorded. One of the details of the fight was that Moses had to stand on top of a hill with the "rod of God in my hand." Everything was OK as long as Moses held up the rod of God. But Moses' arms "got tired," and the rod began to feel very heavy. This was a very small detail; yet it was very important to the outcome of the battle. There was no way Moses could handle this problem alone.

The story goes on to say that two other persons, Aaron and Hur, rolled a stone for Moses to sit on and they stood by him "holding his hands until sunset." Thus, the plan was accomplished, but only because two other persons became "enablers" to Moses.

It is not unusual for a person to need assistance in order to get things done. Think about your own community, your church, your home. Do you know persons or situations where the help of a "manager" or "enabler" would be significant? Are there elderly persons living in your area who can no longer "manage" on their own? Are there children in your community who need guidance? Are there teens who could use some help in putting together the pieces of their lives? List various persons in your school, church, or community who could, in your best estimation, benefit from some enabling, some managing.

Most of you like to be independent; there's nothing wrong with that. But almost every person can use some assistance when it comes to major life plans. Teen lives are busy lives. Details of Action Plans are often overlooked because of the pressure of other details. Good Action Plans can be forgotten because no one checks up on the details to see that certain things are happening when they are supposed to, etc. This is the point where an Action Plan manager can be most valuable to you.

WHO can be an Action Plan manager? There are many possibilities. Another teenager you respect and trust could fill the role. One, or both, of your parents could assist you with one or more of your plans. A church school teacher, youth adviser/counselor, or other church leader might be willing to work with you. A neighbor in whom you have confidence could be an Action Plan manager. Almost any person you feel is dependable and in whom you can confide your Action Plans can do the job.

WHAT will the Action Plan manager do? After you've selected the person(s) to be manager(s) for your Action Plan(s), share the Action Plan Details with them. Provide each with a copy of your Action Plan. Share the Objective, the Action Plan, and the Details from your worksheet. Ask him or her to contact you at certain points in your Action Plan Details. Several strategic times might be:
1. Midway through the Action Plan.
2. At several critical points in the Plan. (Ask your Action Plan manager to contact you at those times.)
3. At the time you complete the plan, for anaylsis and evaluation.

The most important items are the time limits and deadlines you establish. When you work alone, it's easy to ignore deadlines, and they just quietly slip by. However, when someone else is helping you to check details, planning can be much more effective. In fact, you will experience a great sense of satisfaction when you tell your Action Plan manager that you have met certain deadlines, carried out some details, etc.

You may be able to manage several of your Action Plans yourself.

Select Action Plan managers only for those plans that are of greatest significance, that have many details and time limits, and which, if not accomplished, will prevent you from reaching your objective.

It's good to work independently of others and to manage your own affairs as much as possible. But remember it is a wise person who values Action Plans so much that he or she will enlist someone else to help accomplish them. There are many persons who can be a resource to you. Take advantage of what these resource persons (managers/enablers) can offer to your life planning.

As you search for several Action Plan managers to assist you in your life planning, don't forget to include God on your team, too. God is very interested in your plans. You are not too small, unimportant, or insignificant for God to care. God cares for you as a person. He is interested in you—just as you are, and right now! Enlist his support in your future by sharing with him your hopes, dreams, and plans. Ask for his guidance.

Is it what I wanted
it to be?

How Am I Doing?

The grades received for tests taken in school partially answer the question "How am I doing?" Likewise, at the end of each marking period, grades are given which tell a person how he or she did in that subject.

You casually evaluate many aspects of your life. You see a movie, and evaluate it as great, so-so, or perhaps awful! You buy a pizza, and it may be scrumptious, blah, or horrible. You bake a cake, and it's either beautiful to the eye as well as the taste, so-so, or "flat as a pancake" and maybe "hard as a rock." Some clothes you buy fit just right, while others don't. When you drive a car, others evaluate your driving by observing that you're a good driver, a so-so driver, or a menace on the highways! Sometimes you feel good about your home life; at other times you evaluate your home situation and don't feel so good about it.

Life provides many opportunities for evaluation. Much of what you do is evaluated by others. Almost unconsciously you evaluate others. Self-evaluation of your own work is extremely important. When you know how you're doing, or at least have an opinion, you can face evaluation and feedback from others with a greater degree of confidence. Neither self-evaluation or evaluation by others needs to be threatening.

EVALUATING YOUR ACTION PLANS

Evaluation means carefully considering the worth or "value" of what you have done. Evaluating your Action Plans makes it

possible to answer:
- What happened?
- Was it what I wanted?
- Did enough happen to make the plan worthwhile?
- What did I do best?
- What should I have done differently?

In a "for the fun of it" experience, take a lump of Play-Doh and decide what you want to make or do with it. Write down on a piece of paper your plans for that piece of Play-Doh. Keep the paper to yourself. You have five minutes to carry out your plans for that Play-Doh. Do it now!

Now look at what you have created! Show your "masterpiece" to others. Observe their reactions. What did you communicate? Do they know from what you created what is written on that piece of paper in your pocket? Are you proud of what you created? Did you have everything you needed to create what you intended to create?

There are three elements in evaluation. Apply them to your Play-Doh experience.

- Element 1. How well did I organize to carry out my plan(s)? This can be called *structure evaluation*. It deals with the arrangements you make to carry out your Action Plan Details. Jesus pointed to this element when he observed that no person plans to build without first sitting down to figure out what it will cost. (Luke 14:28).
- Element 2. How well did things go? This element is *process evaluation*. It deals with the various things you set up to do in carrying out your Action Plan Details. It deals with the kinds of things to which Proverbs 4:26 (TEV) refers, "Plan carefully what you do. . . ."
- Element 3. What changed? What happened? This is *product evaluation*. It deals with what comes about as a result of having carried out your Action Plan Details. Jesus made several references to this type of evaluation when in Matthew 7:16 (RSV) he said, "You will know them by their fruits," and in Luke 13:9 (RSV) where he said, ". . . if it bears fruit . . . well and good; but if not, you can cut it down."

Let's go back to the Play-Doh. Take a few moments and evaluate what you did with the Play-Doh in terms of these three elements.

Here are some lead questions:

Structure—Did you have the right table, equipment, setting, tools, etc., to make what you wanted to make?

Process   —Did you have enough time to plan?

Did you follow an orderly process to get the result?

Did you know how to make what you wanted to make?

Product   —Did your product look like what you wanted it to be?

Did others recognize it?

Did you communicate what you wanted to communicate?

Do you feel really good about your product?

Would you make this product again?

In most cases, your Action Plan Details Worksheet will provide you with the answers to the various questions asked concerning the three elements of evaluation. For each Action Plan, you will want to have a thorough evaluation upon its completion. Only in this way will you be able to know how well you've done. If you don't complete an Action Plan, be sure and ask the question, "Why?"

On the basis of your evaluation, what do you now feel you ought to do? To each Action Plan, you can respond in one of four ways:

- Repeat the Action Plan, because . . .
- Revise the Action Plan, because . . .
- Replace the Action Plan, because . . .
- Stop the Action Plan (don't ever do it again!), because . . .

Complete the sentence for the type of recommendation you will make to yourself. Some Action Plans are so good that they must be repeated. However, many Action Plans in life planning are the type you do once and then move on to something else. Other plans can be revised and recycled.

You may not be aware of it, but one of the finest examples of evaluation the Christian has is found in the book of Genesis. The planner/builder is none other than God, and in Genesis 1 (TEV), evaluation of each day of creation indicates God "was pleased." Look at verses 12, 18, and 21, at the end of successive days of creation, to see how God's feelings are summed up: "And God was pleased with what he saw." Surely you, too, will want to take time and check out the question: "How am I doing?"

LOOKING AT THE BIG PICTURE

The question "How am I doing?" has both short-range and

long-range aspects. The previous section dealt with the short range. Let's take a look at the long range, or what is sometimes called the "Big Picture."

Auto inspection is required in many states. When you take your car to the garage to be inspected, it is the inspectors' task to look at the whole car, not just one or two parts of it. In order to determine if the car is safe to drive on the road, they must take a look at the "Big Picture." Everything about the car that affects safety factors for the owner/driver must be examined. The inspection takes time, and necessary repairs sometimes take quite a bit of money. However, when the job is completed, you assume the car is ready for the road again.

You've enrolled in many classes and courses during your schooling. In most of them you've been required to take certain tests or examinations. Each test, in and of itself, told you how you were doing for a certain time period or about a small part of the course. It didn't give the "Big Picture" of how you were doing in the whole course. Only when you took the final examination and received a grade which covered the whole course, did you know what the "Big Picture" was telling you.

Since you've been working on this course, you haven't had enough time to work through all your plans, carry them out, and be ready to evaluate them. There is no "Big Picture" to look at yet. However, when that time comes, there are several things at which to look. When you've completed your Action Plan evaluation, you should do the following.

1. Take a look at your Objectives.

   Are you staying within the time frames you set?

   Are you getting the results you wanted from the specific action you stated?

   Is each objective still on target?

   Which objectives have you completed in the last year?

   Do you need to write new objectives, either because you've completed some of them or perhaps because others are out-of-date?

2. Take a look at your Goals.

   During your "younger" years you may want to change goals much more frequently than you will in later years.

   Do your goals still deal with what you want to accomplish?

   Is each goal "on target"?

   Do you feel good about your goals?

   Do your goals excite you? Do you look forward with

excitement to accomplishing them?

Should you rewrite some goals?

3. Take a look at your Purpose Statement.

Does your statement still reflect your thinking about self and life?

Are you satisfied with the statement as written, or should it be revised?

Are all the things you are doing (Objectives and Program Plans) moving you along in your purpose in life?

Now take your Personal Life Line and decide when you will take your first look at your "Big Picture." When will be the most strategic time for you to pause and look at everything you are doing? Select a date (six months, nine months, one year, etc.) and write it on your Life Line. Place the letters "BP" (Big Picture) alongside the date. This will remind you that you want to take a complete look at your life at this point. Remember that you are not locked into the schedule. It can be revised at any point. If an emergency arises, you can look at the "Big Picture" anytime.

Earlier you looked at some verses from the first chapter of Genesis. Now read verse 31 of that chapter. This is how God observed the "Big Picture" just created. In earlier verses in the chapter, God looked at the various steps (Action Plans) of creation. Now it was time to look at everything at the same time. How did God feel?

In conclusion, life planning deals with your future. A ship sets sail on the ocean to reach another port, and its destination is known. From time to time during the voyage, adjustments are made to keep the ship "on target." Keep adjusting, changing, and modifying your life plans in order to get the most out of your life. God bless YOU as you continue your search for direction in life.

Leader's Guide

SESSION 1   WHO IS THE REAL ME?

SESSION GOALS
- Each participant will prepare a Personal Time Line and complete the "Checklist for the REAL Me!"
- Each participant will be prepared to interview others to learn more about himself or herself.
- A biblical focus on the future will be shared.

THE SETTING
Each person will need "elbow room" to write on a piece of newsprint or shelf paper. Adequate wall space needs to be provided, or a floor or tables can be used. Some groups have had a great deal of fun as well as a relaxed experience by working on newsprint on the floor.

Caution: Some wide felt-tip markers will mark through some types of newsprint. Be careful to double the newsprint so that walls or floors in homes or church will not be damaged!

SUPPLIES NEEDED
1. One wide felt-tip marker for each member of the group.
2. One pen or pencil for each member.
3. At least one piece of newsprint for each member. If backing is needed for wall or floor use, provide each person with two pieces. (If newsprint is not available, secure enough wide shelf paper for each group member to have three or four feet.)
4. Masking tape for wall use of newsprint.

5. At least one copy of *The Living Bible.*

LEADER ROLE

• This session calls for much individual work. Your role is to be a guide, an enabler to the process. When questions arise, they will most likely be directed your way. Rather than field questions before the whole group, move to the individual who raised the question and quietly talk with that person. If the question is one which would benefit most of the group, share it with them.

It is important to be aware of each group member's feelings as this process unfolds. Not every person is at the same point of readiness to learn more about "ME"! If a teen is turned off by the process, or is visibly disturbed, do not respond with anger, displeasure, judgmental comments, or disgust. Be gentle and patient. Be a listener. Give evidence of real love and concern by observing what the person is feeling. Respond with warmth and affection. Not every teenager can possibly handle all that is suggested. Help each member to do as much as he or she can do without being threatened or left out. Moments spent with individual teenagers in this way will pay dividends in the future.

• This process can be a fun experience. Help members of your group not to feel weighted down or overwhelmed by the experience.

• Work with each group member concerning persons to interview. If group members are not sure who to interview, assist them by suggesting persons of your acquaintance who could provide helpful feedback. If you know a parent(s) will provide feedback that would be harmful or at least less than helpful, assist this teen to find other persons who might be helpful. If your group members are not used to or are unwilling to do outside work, encourage them to have at least one good interview. Challenge the group members according to your personal knowledge of their capabilities. Most youth groups rarely work to the level of their abilities.

• Bible study. Group members will be working individually most of this session on various steps. Be prepared to guide their thinking for six to eight minutes on this Scripture passage: 1 Corinthians 9:24-27 *(The Living Bible).*

SESSION 2   WHAT IS IMPORTANT?
WHAT DO I VALUE?

SESSION GOALS

- Participants will be able to "sort out" their values . . . what they think is important to them *now*.
- The sense of importance of each group member will be increased.
- Each person will discover his or her heritage.

LEADER ROLE

- If you have an hour or more for Session 2, you may be able to move the group through the three main emphases:
1. What I value—think is important.
2. My accomplishments.
3. My heritage.

If you have less than an hour, concentrate on the first two, and ask group members to complete the section on heritage as an outside assignment.

- Christians seldom talk about what Jesus valued. He considered some things to be highly important. Be prepared to guide your group through this process. Do not provide "answers" for them; however, study the suggested Scriptures (others, too) and prepare your own list in advance of the session. Offer suggestions and help that will provide some clues. If your group is mature and biblically rooted, you will need to give little assistance. However, if your group is young and has little Bible background, you may need to provide much assistance.

- It is your task to monitor the time available for the various steps in each session. Since group members will be doing individual work much of the time, you need to serve as timekeeper for the group.

- Some of these sessions will take more time than you have; so consider opening your home to your group after school, for an evening, or perhaps on a Saturday. Groups which spend time in the home of the leader or a student become much better acquainted. They are more relaxed and have a much greater sense of loyalty and motivation. Consider this as an option for your group.

- Teenagers have differing feelings about what they can do, or have accomplished. Some teens need a "boost" from an adult other than parents and teachers since they rarely get a word of encouragement from anybody. This step is an attempt to help persons see that they have some accomplishments. Whether the deeds are great or small does not matter. What matters is that they become aware of the fact they *are* persons of worth, that they *do* affect the lives of others, and that life *does* have meaning. It is very important that your role be that of an enabler, supporter, and encourager during this session.

• Your group has been asked to share a hug with other group members. Don't be afraid to join in and give a warm hug to every member of your group, male and female! You may need to show the way. Become a caring group!

• Read Matthew 5:1-11 from the Bible. Maybe you'd like to put these verses on newsprint or the chalkboard so all can read together; or give each person a mimeographed copy if individual Bibles are not available.

SESSION 3   CAN YOU HEAR WHAT I'M REALLY SAYING?

SESSION GOALS
• All group members will examine the subject of communications.
• Each person will look at his or her responsibilities and how he or she feels about them!
• Help each person begin the process of "sorting out" what he or she believes.

THE SETTING
Almost any room at church or home will be suitable for this session. All that's needed is a comfortable place to do some writing and talking. If you use triads in the communications game, they can be located in several rooms if they're available. If you do the communications game as a total group, one room will be sufficient.

SUPPLIES NEEDED
At least one sheet of paper, one pencil, and the student's book are needed for each group member. One onion will be used by the group.

LEADER ROLE
• As in the past two sessions, most of Session 3 will call for individual work. When teens use the book, you should be available

for questions and assistance where needed. If your group consists of post highs, the section on "Responsibilities" is not applicable.

• How much time do you have? That, as well as the pace at which your group works, will help you decide whether you can attempt the three goals or not. The most important step in this session is the third, "My Faith." If you have time for only one other, deal with the first step on "How Well Do I Communicate?" and assign the "Responsibilities" step as outside work.

• You've now spent two or three sessions dealing with the basic question: Who am I? It's hard work, but well worth the time. Encourage your group to continue to "look for the real me" by searching more deeply and doing it often. Use the following exercise to help get the point across. Have an onion and a small paring knife available. The onion should be at least two or three inches in diameter. Try to get one with plenty of "tear juice." Let each member take off a layer. A close grouping over a table so all can see (and cry) will help illustrate the statement. At long last, you'll find the heart of the onion.

• The communications game can be a lot of fun as well as a helpful learning tool. Be sure you understand it before the session begins, so that valuable time isn't wasted "spinning wheels."

• If you have time, you may want to discuss as a group some of the "I Wonder About This . . ." items. Also, you can prepare a simple and brief closing devotional on the mustard seed verse, Matthew 17:30.

SESSION 4   WHAT'S LIFE ALL ABOUT, ANYWAY?

Session 4 is a challenge. It is not easy. Study the material and decide if your group is ready to "tackle" the subject of life purpose. If your group is too young and/or immature, you may want to omit this session and move on to Session 5. Be sure to come back and complete Session 4 at a later date since life purpose is significant.

SESSION GOAL

• Each member will begin the process of thinking about, and perhaps writing out, a life-purpose statement.

- Extra assistance will be given to those who want to work further on their life-purpose statement.

LEADER ROLE

- The best way to prepare for this session is to "do it yourself." Read the text, and sort out your own "mission in life." The very group you now lead may be a part of that mission.

- In preparation, read the Scripture references given below at the beginning of the session. Be ready to share them with the group. If you select the creation role play, perhaps you will want to read selections from Genesis in the group before the role play takes place. The references are as follows:

> Jesus said: "Do not start worrying . . ." Matthew 6:31 (TEV).
> Writer of Ecclesiastes: ". . . nothing new under the sun" Ecclesiastes 1:9 (RSV).
> Creation account: Genesis 1 and 2

Search your newspapers and magazines for recent articles about people who have either "given up" or who have no sense of purpose or mission. Look for others that tell of people who didn't give up, who have found a mission in life. You can share these with your group in addition to those listed in the book. Attempt to involve the group in a meaningful discussion.

- There are three different role plays suggested. Most groups will have time for only one; if you have a longer session, perhaps you can do two. Select the one which best fits your group. Another approach to the role play is to secure two or three group members who will, in advance of the session, select the best one for the group and lead them in it.

- The empty table exercise is optional. If you have time, do it; if not, mention what it is and move on. If you elect to do it, help your teens get everything on the table, including big and small items from their lives. Many of the so-called "little people" have real purpose in their lives. They don't have to be "great" leaders in the community or church; they don't need to be successful in business; neither do they need to "make the headlines." Identify two persons you know personally who have found meaning in life; do this in advance of the class session. It will be helpful to share your selections with the group. Group members will "catch on" from what you have done.

- Some members will be ready to attempt to write a statement. Offer your assistance to any member who wants individual help during the week. If some of your group or class aren't motivated to do this, meet with them separately while others work on their purpose statements. For those who don't wish to prepare a purpose statement, perhaps another role play could be done.

• Close the session with a significant prayer about what you have been doing.

• Some sample life-planning purpose statements might include:
—God calls me to be a witness. (The source, or cause, of witness is lodged in God.)
—The needs of humanity compel me to pursue scientific exploration. (In this case, the needs of other human beings are responsible for the "why.")

SESSION 5   BUT I THOUGHT ... !

SESSION GOALS

• Each member of the group will understand the meaning of the term "assumption."
• Individual work on writing out assumptions will begin.

LEADER ROLE

• By now you have a general idea of how much time your group or class will need to work through exercises, etc. Study Session 5 in its entirety to determine which options best fit your situation.

• Of the items available in this session, the following are "musts":
—Definition
—At least two of the Situations. If you have time for only two, select Situation 2 (Moses) and one other. If you have time for only one, use Situation 2.
—At least one of the exercises.
—Four categories of assumptions. If time permits, do the follow-up exercise.
—Individual work. At least get it started. Select the best options for your group, and work within your time framework.

• The story of Moses is used to point out that assumptions have been around a long time. They played a part in the lives of biblical characters. If you have a special interest—and time—other Scripture passages can be used as illustrations of this point.

• The subject of assumptions is not easy to grasp. Take time to encourage your group to see that this phenomenon is a normal part of everyday life. It's also an important part of life planning.

• Some of your group members may have a "tough time" with this session, If so, make arrangements for several of them to get together with you during the week. It is *assumed* that every leader greatly cares for every member of the group. Check out that assumption!

This session is left "open-ended," since we have *assumed* your group or class members will be doing individual work. Have a closing prayer and a Scripture reading (Matthew 6:25-33), sing a song, or do whatever is appropriate for your group at that time.

• After you have studied Session 5, if the meaning of the term "assumption " is still unclear to you, talk to your pastor about it. Ask for his or her help in preparing to teach this session.

SESSION 6   SOME REAL CONCERNS

SESSION GOALS

• Each participant will understand the meaning of the term "Area of Concern."
• Each member will have sorted out his or her concerns, selected the top six, and decided which is number one.

SUPPLIES NEEDED

Tinker Toys, building blocks, or both. *(Check with your church nursery before purchasing these items.)*

LEADER ROLE

• It is important to do all that is suggested for this session. Study the entire lesson and assign time limits to the various pieces in the lesson.

• Place the four categories of concerns (problems, needs, issues, and opportunities/challenges) in big letters on newsprint or the chalkboard. Write the definition under each. Briefly deal with the questions related to each.

• The Peters, Jameses, and Johns of history all had concerns, too.

Help your group understand that those in the Bible had many concerns, acted on them, and often faced some difficult circumstances as a result. Study the Scripture in advance of the class, so you will have some answers available to "prime the pump" if necessary.

• The group you lead has now been together for a month and a half if you've used all the sessions to date. Many things have happened to your group. In a light vein, try to pull from members of the group some of their concerns from this short period of time.

• Use Tinker Toys or regular building blocks *(different sizes and shapes)* to illustrate the need for a goal. Do not participate in this exercise. Be an observer and take notes. Share some of your observations at the end of the exercise. All of this is a "pointer" to the next session on goal writing. Goals become the "stars to which you hitch your wagons." Concerns are difficult to deal with when they stand alone or are disorganized. Drive this point home in preparation for Session 7.

• Close with an appropriate prayer.

(Take a week off before beginning the next session. For the sake of variety, offer a different style of program; or perhaps a complete change of scenery, style, and/or content would be most beneficial.)

• Advance work with a tape recorder is recommended prior to Session 7. Study the Leader's Guide and make appropriate assignments in order to guarantee available material for the session.

SESSION 7   ESTABLISHING PERSONAL GOALS

Almost everyone has some goals in life toward which he or she is working. Writing out these goals, revising them, or establishing new goals is a most important step in life planning.

Understanding what a goal is, as well as what it is not, is extremely important. Study the definition as well as the examples provided in the student material. Many people talk about goals which aren't really goals at all; in most cases, they are plans or strategies which are instrumental in reaching a goal, but not the goal itself.

Goals provide a long-range dimension to a person's approach to life. They offer both challenge and excitement to you as you figure out how to reach them.

SESSION GOAL

- Each member will have written at least one goal statement for his or her life, based on his or her number one area of concern; more, if possible.

SUPPLIES NEEDED

1. Several tape recorders (in advance of this session).
2. Newsprint and markers or chalkboard and chalk.
3. Personal Life Lines from Session 1.

LEADER ROLE

- At least one week in advance of this session, enlist two or three group members to use a tape recorder and have a few people tape their responses to the question: "What are your goals in life?" If no tape recorders are available, interviewers can write down the responses; however, a recording will provide exact statements rather than what the interviewer thought they said. Discuss these responses during the session. Use the recordings only as illustrations of what people think are goals for life; do not encourage judgmental statements about what anyone has said. Some may be quite accurate; others may not be goals at all.

- If you're following this process personally, write a goal for yourself that meets all the criteria.

- When writing goals, sometimes it is helpful for group members to work in teams (two or three to a team). If this will be helpful to your group, form teams that will provide a good support system while writing the goals.

- Be available to individuals and/or teams while they write goal statements. Do not write their goals for them. However, be sensitive to individual needs. Some may need much more help than others. Provide just the right amount of assistance needed to help each person complete the task.

- Near the end of the session, refer your group members back to the Personal Life Line they created in Session 1. As they establish goals, help group members place them somewhere on the line between the "You Are Here" point, and the end of the Life Line that they have chosen. If they have fifty years yet to live, then most of these goals will probably occur very close to the "You Are Here" point on the line. Help them to make these goals visible as well as to add new ones, cancel out those which are accomplished, etc.

- In closing, you might want to tie it all together with a Scripture passage which reflects goal achievement or striving to accomplish something. Two suggestions are:

Philippians 3:14
1 Corinthians 9:24

SESSION 8   SETTING SOME OBJECTIVES

Discovering objectives to help you reach goals can be exciting. Be sure you understand the meaning of objectives before you lead the session. The best way to handle this is to write some objectives for yourself. Writing objectives is a very important step in planning. They tend to provide time frames for your life which become self-imposed disciplines for your future.

SESSION GOAL
- Each member will have written at least one or more objectives related to a specific life goal.

LEADER ROLE
- If you're following this process personally, write an objective for yourself that meets all the criteria.
- If you can find a picture of a huge rock, it would be good to hang it in a conspicuous place and refer to it as you work through the session material.
- If working in pairs was helpful to your group in the last session, you may want to follow the same procedure. If individual work is better, encourage them to work alone.
- A sample objective for the feeding of the five thousand might be: Within one or two hours, obtain enough food for five thousand persons to be fed one meal.
- Make yourself available to pairs or individuals as they work on objectives. It might be helpful to the group if, when a member has written an objective which meets all criteria, it could be shared with all of them (if the writer is in agreement). This process might provide some encouragement and incentive that "it can be done."
- Close with some thoughts on the feeding of the five thousand, as recorded in John 6:1-13.

SESSION 9   ACTION!!

You've now arrived at the place where almost everyone wants to be most of the time—the "doing" state! Most people would rather "do something now" and ask "why?" later. This course has reversed that process by taking you through a series of steps which asked many "why?" questions, and now leads you to the "doing." Although not immediately apparent, the product that can emerge in young lives can be far more satisfactory and meaningful.

Action Plans are basically what young people will actually *do* with their lives. Finding the right—and best—plan(s) is very important. *You* are a *very important* part of the process in your role as group leader. So is God. Encourage the members of your group to talk to God on a regular basis about their future—and their planning.

SESSION GOAL

- Each member will have written at least one action plan, more if possible.

LEADER ROLE

- You are now a builder, adding building blocks in an orderly fashion. A diagram of what you have done thus far would look like this.

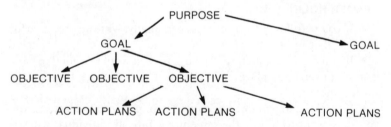

This is just an illustration. There could be more goals, more objectives, and many more action plans than indicated in this diagram. If you think it would help your group to see the diagram, share it with them on newsprint or chalkboard.

- Try to identify some personal action plans on which you are currently working. Are there others you'd like to be working on? Share them with your group at an appropriate time, if you'd like.
- Depending on the size of your group, you may be able to use only one of the "practice" brainstorm experiences. It is *very* important that young people (and adults) learn the fact that other persons can be valuable resources to them in life planning. We live in community; we

can be supportive and helpful; we are interdependent!

• Some possible action plans for the objective about being a millionaire are:

- —I will take a quick course on stocks and bonds.
- —I will get a full-time job—quick! (one that pays well!)
- —I will go to school in order to get a better paying job.
- —I will rob a bank (this would help with the savings account—maybe!)
- —I will enlist others to join with me in this objective.
- —I will inherit some money.
- —I will write a book.
- —I will invent something, like a substitute for gasoline!
- —And on and on.

• Form small groups and have each bring all their ideas for Action Plans to the total group. Some may be funny or ridiculous (like rob a bank!), but put down all contributions. Then when this process has been completed for the illustrations, use the same small groups to sort out the *best* plan for each member in that group. After the best idea has been designated as an Action Plan, any other idea which appears to be helpful and realistic can become an additional Action Plan with which to reach the objective. The number of Action Plans which can be selected is limited only by the amount of time, resources, and motivation the person wants to give toward accomplishing this objective.

• In closing, stress the importance of being open to the will of God in doing life planning. God cares. God cares about young people and their future. Encourage them to make their future a matter of meaningful prayer. If members of your group have progressed to the place where they can pray for each other individually, close with this approach. It will enhance your group's life.

SESSION 10   DETAILS!! DETAILS!!

Since you are a leader, little needs to be said about details. Proper attention to details usually enhances a lesson or program; details which are neglected usually cause poor results. You know that. The same is true about our lives. If we fail to handle adequately the little things about our lives, trouble and disappointment may lie ahead. God was so concerned about his Action Plan to save a small part of his creation from destruction by the flood that he gave specific details about its construction, and they are still recorded many thousands of years later. That's why the story of Noah and the ark will be helpful to the understanding of Action Plan Details.

SESSION GOALS

• Action Plan Details' outline for the story of Noah and the ark will be produced.

• Each member will have written at least one set of Action Plan Details, related to his or her number one objective.

SUPPLIES NEEDED

1. Record player.
2. Bill Cosby's record which includes the story of Noah and the ark. Record title: "Bill Cosby Is a Very Funny Fellow. Right!" Produced by Allan Sherman and Roy Silver. Warner Brothers Record #1518.
3. Each student will need a copy of the Details Worksheet at the end of this session.
4. Set of blueprints.

LEADER ROLE

• If you can't locate the Cosby record, enlist some members of your group to find it. They could check with the school library, friends who have record collections, etc. The three excerpts are amusing and will provide a humorous introduction to the session.

• Have one or two of your members secure a set of blueprints and share them with the group. Old blueprints can be secured from builders, contractors, etc.

• Take the time to have the Scripture read in its entirety (Genesis 6:5-22; 7:1-10). Ask several students to prepare in advance to read it to the group.

• Action Plan Details of the Noah's ark story might look like this:

Who?   —Noah and his family. God was also involved.

When?   —Begin to build it right now. Plan would be completed after forty days and nights of rain, and a "drying out" period.

Where?   —Build it somewhere in the Tigris-Euphrates Valley (most likely).

How?   —Noah and his sons had to build the ark themselves.

Much, much work was required. Lumber had to be
secured. All building supplies had to be brought to the
site. Food was secured. Animals and birds had to be
located and brought on board. Etc., etc.

What will be different? —All human beings, except for Noah
and his family, were destroyed. All animals and bird
life, except those in the ark, were destroyed. God
purged his earth of the "wickedness of the day."

Many, many more details could be added. Help your group to
imagine the whole plan. It was God's plan, and Noah was to carry out
the details. The ark was a huge structure. Translate the biblical details
into contemporary lengths and widths. Secure details from a Bible
dictionary in your church or pastor's library if you don't have one.

• Details need to be worked out for each Action Plan. Help your
group members complete at least one Action Plan.

• It might be appropriate to close this session by thinking about
the story of Noah and God's intervention in the world. Use the third
excerpt from the Cosby record titled: "Noah: Me and You, Lord."
Then talk about God's later intervention in the world in the coming of
Jesus Christ.

SESSION 11   SOME ASSISTANCE, PLEASE!

From time to time, all of us are "guilty" of either forgetting or
ignoring important details. We feel we can "take care of them later";
often this simply means they never get done. The purpose of this
session is to stress the importance of securing "other-than-self"
assistance in carrying out the details of Action Plans. It is not
necessary to secure an Action Plan manager (other than self) for
every Action Plan. However, significant plans should have an Action
Plan manager, selected by the life planner, in order to "guarantee"
their completion.

Depending on the amount of time you have to give, perhaps you
could be an Action Plan manager for some of the members of your
group.

SESSION GOAL

• Each group member will understand the concept and will

identify at least one person as a potential Action Plan manager.

LEADER ROLE

• You are nearing the end of the course. This session is not lengthy; you may want to combine it with Session 12 on evaluation (if pressed for time). Also, there may be "catch-up" work to be done by members of your group. Slow the pace.

• You may want to discuss with the group how to make contacts when securing Action Plan managers. Here are some suggestions for youth to use in talking with potential managers.

    1. Carefully explain what life planning is all about. Briefly outline the steps that have brought you to the place where a manager is needed.

    2. Explain what an Action Plan is and what you hope it will do.

    3. Interpret the role of the Action Plan manager.

    4. Openly share why you have selected this person to help you with the plan, i.e., you trust him or her, his or her dependability and / or qualifications as a resource person, etc.

    5. Secure a commitment on his or her part to work with you.

• Be prepared to offer suggestions of names to group members who can't think of anyone "on their own."

• Being all alone is a terrible feeling. Being cared for or supported is a wonderful, warm feeling. Close with some thoughts about some of the warm, supportive promises Jesus made. Jesus said, "I am with you always" (Matthew 28:20, *The Living Bible*). Another is, "Where two or three are gathered in my name, there am I in the midst of them" (Matthew 18:20, RSV). Use other verses if you prefer.

SESSION 12   HOW AM I DOING?

Evaluation is the key to your future. Those who pause from time to time to ask the question "How am I doing?" are indeed wise. Reviewing "what I have done" and "how well I did it" will provide a wealth of information with which to decide the next steps of your life. Teenagers are busy; they have many pressures with which to contend; it is not "normal" for teenagers to stop and see how well they are doing. Most of them dislike tests and other checkpoints because they are often threatening. Therefore, it is the purpose of Session 12 to attempt to convince them of the logic of pausing from time to time to ask the question "How am I doing?"

At this point in the course you may not have any Action Plans ready for evaluation. Therefore, the exercise suggested in the session is of utmost importance and should be handled in its entirety.

SESSION GOAL

- Each group member will understand why evaluation is important and acquire a tool which will be helpful in evaluating Action Plans.
- Each group member will understand the need for at least a "once-a-year" evaluation of the "Big Picture."

THE SETTING

- Space for individual and group work is needed. Table space will also be needed for the Play-Doh experience.

SUPPLIES NEEDED

- Play-Doh is needed in a quantity sufficient for each person to have an adequate amount for the exercise.
- Each student should have one of his or her Action Plan Details Worksheets available.
- Each member's Personal Life Line should be available.
- A pen or pencil for each member.
- 3" x 5" cards, or small pieces of paper.
- Bibles.
- Tables.

LEADER ROLE

- Be sure every person in your group understands the meaning of the word "evaluation."
- The Play-Doh exercise is very important. Build it up. Attempt to get every member to write on the slip of paper a real challenge to make something from the Play-Doh.
- As you examine the three elements, be sure to read the Scripture verses in their entirety.
- Deal with the four possible responses to an Action Plan evaluation. In most cases, teens will not repeat Action Plans because of the rapid movement of their lives. Change is apparent every day. Most Action Plans will not be repeated without some modification.
- Deal with the various verses in Genesis 1 which refer to God's

evaluation of each day of the creation. (For example, see Genesis 1:10.)

• To deal with the "Big Picture" will not take a great amount of time. Budget your available time between sharing the concept of short-range evaluation and the "Big Picture."

• There are many other illustrations that can be used to explain the "Big Picture." When building a house, you can evaluate the various steps in the construction process; however, when it is completed, you can look at the total picture and evaluate. Planting a garden, growing a house plant, and building a car are other illustrations which can be used.

• Your group members should mark on their Personal Life Lines when they will take their first "Big Picture" look. Have them mark a "BP" at that point. If you will have ongoing relationships with this same group, it might be good to remind them of this agreement later on.

• As you evaluate the course, be sure you or someone else takes notes on the experience. You may want to share these with your board of Christian education or youth committee.

• Conclude this session with a celebration. By now you should have a rather close-knit group. Perhaps you will want to celebrate with a service of Communion. If the group has developed to the point where members can pray for one another individually, this might have great meaning as you close this course of study.